JAKE HAWKEY was born ... ...on and grew up in Thamesmead, Plumstead, and Woolwich. He studied art at the University of Westminster and poetry at Queen's University in Belfast, where he currently lives and works. His chapbook *Breeze Block* appeared from Lumpen in 2020. *But & Though* is his debut collection.

Also by Jake Hawkey

Breeze Block

Jake Hawkey

But & Though

PICADOR

First published 2025 by Picador
an imprint of Pan Macmillan
The Smithson, 6 Briset Street, London EC1M 5NR
EU representative: Macmillan Publishers Ireland Ltd, 1st Floor,
The Liffey Trust Centre, 117–126 Sheriff Street Upper,
Dublin 1, D01 YC43
Associated companies throughout the world
www.panmacmillan.com

ISBN 978-1-0350-4810-6

Copyright © Jake Hawkey 2025

The right of Jake Hawkey to be identified as the
author of this work has been asserted by him in accordance
with the Copyright, Designs and Patents Act 1988.

All rights reserved. No part of this publication may be reproduced,
stored in a retrieval system, or transmitted, in any form, or by any means
(electronic, mechanical, photocopying, recording or otherwise)
without the prior written permission of the publisher.

The Notes & Acknowledgements on page 95 constitute
an extension of this copyright page.

Pan Macmillan does not have any control over, or any responsibility for,
any author or third-party websites referred to in or on this book.

1 3 5 7 9 8 6 4 2

A CIP catalogue record for this book is available from the British Library.

Printed and bound by CPI Group (UK) Ltd, Croydon, CR0 4YY

This book is sold subject to the condition that it shall not, by way of
trade or otherwise, be lent, hired out, or otherwise circulated without
the publisher's prior consent in any form of binding or cover other than
that in which it is published and without a similar condition including
this condition being imposed on the subsequent purchaser.

Visit **www.picador.com** to read more about all our books
and to buy them. You will also find features, author interviews and
news of any author events, and you can sign up for e-newsletters
so that you're always first to hear about our new releases.

This book is for my grandfather
Brian Hugh Ferris
1940–2012
for his forbearance,
for believing I'd come good

for Eric Kearsley
1930–2019
for gifting me the means
to study poetry formally

for children of alcoholics everywhere
& all families in the grip of addiction

Contents

1

First Outing   3

Fake Ransom Note   5

Prescription   6

Fathers & Sons   9

Dad's still in a coma so I'm sent   10

The Objects   12

ICU   14

Lenny   16

London & Sons   17

The Wrappers   19

Off the Back of a Lorry   20

The Remaining Garys   21

Routines   24

Sticks Not Twigs   28

Flights   30

2

Working-Class Boy in a Shower Cap   37

The Boy Asking a Question   40

The Boy Selling Houses   42

The Boy Selling Beds 44

Bobby 46

Calling Nanny P 47

The Prince 49

Dirty 50

Wok-A-Moley 52

Popular Boy 53

Houdini 54

Toy Town 56

Juliet Says to Her Nurse, the City is a Bruise 57

O Girl 58

Brahms & Liszt 60

The Girl Who Grew up to Drive Ambulances 62

Sweeper 64

But & Though 65

3

Happy Hour 69

The Present 71

Booby Trap 73

Spaghetti Western, Alphabetti Spaghetti, Spaghetti to Forgetti Your Regretti, Spaghetti & a Whole Fist 74

The Passover 77

Silent Prayer in Eau Claire 78

Potluck   80

The Understudies   81

Glint of Promise   82

The Professional Peanut Butter Taster   84

We Disagree on Sabrina for a Girl   86

Friday Night Drift   88

Saturday   90

For My Daughter to Come   91

Birthday Suicide Letter   92

Notes & Acknowledgements   95

*It was so long ago — I remember it still —
that I was felled from the forest's edge,
ripped up from my roots.*

[. . .]

*And as we stood there, weeping, a long while
fixed in our station, the song ascended
from those warriors.*

from Dream of the Rood

I

My ideal weight is 205, actually.

Philip Seymour Hoffman

First Outing

I remember
how the iron
seemed to sweat
& heave its steam
around the room
disproportionately
when you first quit,
as if all of time
was Sunday
& everything
was so English
it hurt,
cut-glass
accent of
the news
& I thought
I'd made it worse
insisting you went
to Alcoholics
Anonymous
where you had to
stand up & say
your name like
a new synonym
for powerlessness;
you had to wear

a badge. Dry
three months
that first time,
coming off
spirits, then
blaming the spirits
so switching to
cider — no more
broken glass but
slight tin cans bent
double as your body
becoming bloated
from the extra sugar;
you were sweeter,
had us convinced

Fake Ransom Note

Duckers & divers keep some happiness in a pocket
to soften the way down. Be good to people. I will call
from every telephone box in the country of my mother's
birth & walk the thoroughfares of all the club-footed
towns, still finding them surprising. To stop her drinking,
I made a ransom note with gluey words from headlines
demanding she quit or else her children would be taken;
it just meant I ate bread & silence alone for two days,
grounded, *the saucy sod*. Once I sent a great invention
to a chocolate bar company & they replied in writing
'the bar is already too high'. Nobody was ever a toilet
cleaner in their former life, only a king or a queen.
Only once did I do something that meant something,
I'm sure of it, but I can't remember what it was

Prescription

1. Blocked

I was just a boy when Mum was drunk
every night & I thought that meant
she did not love me. The unloved
still rents the rooms of my body,
working to teach the loved me
how unworthy of life I am,
presenting unreturned calls or
unreceived invitations as evidence.

Who hired this grey prosecution?
Mum's patched up in the hospital;
they remove only traces & symptoms.
She drank so much she began to erase
her own memory of herself
— which self? The loved

2. The Nights

I have spent nights in this world watching
you fall asleep into black bean noodles,
hair in your mouth, eyes closed for business,
sunbathing on the beaches of the abyss.
Your love is a haul of mirrors buried below dirt.
Now all we share is a small council house.
What happened to you, this woman so proud,
who tied up my boots, cut my hair with a bowl?

Some day soon I'll be moving your furniture,
covering stains on a newly rented carpet,
spreading plastic sheets over your mattress,
checking the alarm & if the nurse can hear it.
Some day soon I'll be fixing your nappy there,
saying I love you, following the script

3. You're a Joke

What did the fifth commandment
say to the other nine? For Chrissake,
tidy your rooms! What did Moses say
to the firefighter trying to douse
the burning bush? You wouldn't
know God from a flame if He licked
a little red across your cheek.

What use is love if it's conditional?
A mother's love, a father's love,
a young girl in Nazareth
hiding a bulge – her love,
pure as an angel's. Breast milk
dribbling, wetting skinny straw,
an unfinished season

Fathers & Sons

after Tom Leonard

I built a foal with four loo rolls, a shoebox
& a birthday candle for its silky neck. I build
it here again. My gift to you at parents' evening:
the teacher makes a presentation; you smile, nod,
put it in the bin as we leave. I'm a paperboy folded,
feeling the streets around us & pulling my weight.

You in the salt air of Blackpool, with steamy Mother
in dance halls, in Church's brogues. Our shared taste
for motorhomes beyond our means, further & farther.

We sell my first guitar when the internet is young,
making one hundred pounds & did I love you
wrapping our shipment like an Egyptian queen.
You cannot extract our money from the screen.
You're so embarrassed I say *Let's send it anyway*

Dad's still in a coma so I'm sent

beyond the hospital doors for five bags of chips,
three cod, plenty of salt & vinegar, mayonnaise
for my little sister. When I return, Dad's mother
— whose name I have always loved, Pamela,
& whose mother's name I have always loved more,
Elizabeth May West — says *'ark, put these chips
below his nose, see if he don't wake up then.*
Hahaha, applause in the family room.

When the others were away at football
I was all hers as we peeled potatoes
& Dad broke the silence falling through the door
with mud up his back & news of the final score.
Mum's chips with fried eggs when all was good.
Look at me, I've found the biggest chip in the world!

*

I ask a blonde Irish nurse if geezers go to heaven
& she gifts me two handfuls of rectangular shampoo
like it's mayonnaise or ketchup. I rub it into Mum's scalp
over a sink in the family room, whoosh it up into a twirl
like a Smurf's hat & send a picture to the group: *LOL!*
Dad's being switched off tomorrow, so his best friend
takes Mum to an off-licence; a bottle of Strongbow
in a blue plastic shroud bubbles below the basin.

1 a.m. we walk out the automatic doors for a smoke
where newborns set sail smelling of peach & sawdust.
The bruised fruits of Denmark Hill, Camberwell & Brixton
glide in unconscious, plastic funnels mining into every orifice.
3 a.m. we're still trying to sleep on gashed ICU settees &
Mum's a girl again: *Will he still love me when he wakes up?*

The Objects

Plastic flowers do not understand the first thing about dying. The nurse on this ward bouncing away in mauve pumps while daydreaming of the upcoming weekend understands that he is dying, but he's just one part of her day, a day she makes merry as she leans into the seconds to make good the hours. He's soon to be another statistic, but he is still my father while the machine blows oxygen into his lungs.

I sit & talk to the man my mother has kept clean-shaven, this man who probably cannot hear what I am saying: his brain-stem is dead, everything is guess. When they run their final tests, they pour water into his ear like a closing plea for the sea to wake him, making me a nipper again with my forearms wrapped around his gigantic neck as he descends into the baby-blue depths on a hotel front in Alicante, a submarine with its bottlenose sidekick. They crease the pages of his eyes to gather dumb clouds & their givings, but it chooses not to rain, doesn't blink or drizzle. No movement or response registered — *Sorry, there is nothing more we can do* — so they move the horizon until it's flat with change. It's a long line, a poet trying to find the words, so of course I ask the nurse *Will you let me see his feet one more time?* She whistles up the thin white sheet like it's a parachute, like a pale coward facing away while speaking their final testimony, & his distinctly crooked toes form the very last image of my father before the curtain is drawn.

When the doctor told us it's just a matter of time, Mum ran to the bed wailing like a siren for Dad to wake up now, please, stop pretending, this joke isn't funny anymore, get up, & when I tried to comfort her I was just another object in the room, but when my eldest brother, Lenny – who had not spent the years telling her off or trying to save her from herself – sailed in, as handsome as ever, like pure light repeating, a hymn, taking his own mother into his arms – *it's okay, it's okay* – the room believed him

ICU

The obese book I finish says
early sibling & parental death's
statistically more common in
families experiencing problems
with problem drinking, but after
Dad died from a broken heart,
the cardiologists fail to mention
your vodka orange, the wrestling,
the launching of heels towards
Dad's face while he smashed the
garden gate Grandad built into
two, four, six, eight – who
do we appreciate? – pieces.
What's up, Doc? No
problemo!

When we pulled the plug
because his brain was mush,
you & I both left for a smoke.
Sensing my hostility, you kept
your distance & words empty,
like a weightless coffee cup in
the movements of a soap actress,
all the unsung melodies. Going
through what's left, there's Dad's
old phone with your number
stored as both Boozy & Woozy.
Despite being dizzy, he still
loved & loves you – to say
his heart wasn't up to it,
though, too easy

Lenny

Last night, I sat on the edge of my bed & wept.

Some claim my name from the Hebrew,
transliterated into Latin script as *Ya'aqov'el – May God*

protect. As a kid, I wandered & watched the iron spit
a small pool onto your FCUK t-shirt. I watched you change,

leave me unprotected. You weren't afraid to make them wait,
& the club would often end in a good fight, wouldn't it?

One night, six beefy bouncers led you down an alleyway,
having had enough by then too.
                                        The house lit up with calls,

Mum sat aching, Dad sped to be with you at the hospital.

Yes, I know why you stay out late, where all this begins, why
we need to be loved so ferociously. Sit here now,
                                                   stay with me

London & Sons

Long dog in the sun
three metres from a woman
rustling sleeping bag

*

You sit at the back
of the bus
like mini kings

throwing snappers
at the windows
at the long ears

of the elderly
in their seats
never looking back

O emperors!
you are only
caesar salads

cut by sixty sporks
so no one in particular
can be blamed

you're tyres in the Thames
masquerading
as monsters

with soft underbellies
& your sisters plucking hairs
from out of your bridge backs

your strength is your weakness
your weakness is your strength
can you believe that?

& if you dream of somebody
do they dream of you?
& if you dream

of autumn
will it fall for you?
do you ever kick up the leaves?

The Wrappers

On stilts, the McDonald's sign is visible
from all positions around the estate:
between washing flapping on balconies
or at the heel of a fleet of Royal Mail vans.

When our father died, my youngest brother Ronnie
ordered Maccy D's every morning to be delivered
to our door by a driver who had picked it up
less than four hundred metres from our house,

less than one full lap of a running track.
He is grateful, tips & this goes on for weeks.
Dad died from hypercholesterolemia, hypertension,
a heart attack. Ronnie's breakfast depresses me.

The wrappers sit bent in the bin, sulking melancholic
brown pools of grease like tidy lagoons, no bathers.
The same brown as the letter received about Dad's
kidneys & their new lease of life in another dad

of a distant family. Mum was glad to get that letter,
but it kept her in bed for another couple of weeks.
The game shows of Saturday fend off the silence.
Only the deliveries open the door to sunlight

Off the Back of a Lorry

A picture of you on a hot balcony in a white t-shirt
with the print *There'll always be an England* & Gazza
in tears, applauding up to the crowd. I drove home

the night you passed away & a song came on the radio —
Vieni Qui or Come Here & this is how men like you go,
isn't it Dad? With three hundred pounds in a bank account

& a bedroom of box-fresh trainers that fell off the back.
I didn't know what else to get! you said as you bopped out
the tattooist's on Margate beach with the Cross of Saint George

on your calf, a close French crop & sweating McMilkshake.
Our home town was built by concreting over marshland.
I'll miss how dirty you were all the time.

Are you upstairs, delivering parcels & catching what falls?
Or sat beside the Ark of the Covenant in the twelfth Lalibela?
You were my church built into a great rock, you were its shade

The Remaining Garys

They gave me my dead father's knitted jumper
& told me it was lucky, to visit the bookies
with it on, to choose a horse in title closest
to his name or character, & so I did,
& this horse fell at the final fence,
& I heard later on that it was put
down, that no horse was ever
named that name again,
nor wore his pattern
of sorbet pink,
coin bronze

*

They say you have a better chance
of having a heart attack on
your settee than winning
the lottery, but that's how
Dad actually died so
those are good odds
for me buying
a baby-pink
slip

*

My father was a young father,
my father was young when
he passed. My little
brother was a cub,
become a bear

*

Mumma Bear says
just try your best
& that really
is the best
advice

*

Big Poppa Bear says

I was coming home in the kebab . . .
         no
                  I mean cab
Haha
hahahahaha
hahahahahahaha
hahahahahah
Ahahahahahaha
hahahahaha
Hahahahahaha
haaa

we laugh so much Dad joins in

everyone gives up on the story

Routines

1. Vampire

I have so much self-doubt
I doubt one day I will see myself in the mirror.
I seem to remember liking myself more when I looked.
I could inhabit the goodness of a moment,
to feel the thick white socks on my feet
while sitting nowhere in particular.
I'm mature enough to know
some of this is my fault.

One morning driving us to school,
Mum realized we did not know the sequence of the alphabet
or the order of the months of the calendar year,
so we would sing them back to her there in the car
with clean white teeth & our noses pointing in the air.
If she'd been breathalysed we'd have been taken into care

2. So Fresh & So Clean

They washed my mouth out with soap
whenever I spoke a naughty word. Fuck them.
Usually the threat of Dad would stop me,
but not the day Mum held me & my slippery tongue
as a veil of silence descended over us both.
It was like she didn't want to do it but had to,
the way you feel before cleaning a bathroom.
My mouth tasted like a perfume factory

the whole day at school. Once I lied to her
about having cleaned my teeth before leaving
so she drove in & made me brush them in the Girls'.
Sometimes I think my unspoken rebellion
is to keep my teeth dirty & sleep with hot breath.
It's also a self-sabotage plot where I am the villain

3. Snowball Fights

You would have a snowball in your hand
when I got home from school, before the glossy
evening news, ready to throw; & sometimes
they'd become glass shards, Dad's screeching,
slippy tyres speeding away from the cul-de-sac.
The ingredients filled the vegetable drawer
of our fridge: advocaat, lemonade, green limes,
paper umbrellas & you would get so lost & cold

packing & mounding snowballs, Mum, you'd pretend
your palms weren't rose-pink marble. My mother lies,
my mother makes me doubt my own hands. I pretend too,
closing my eyes, imagining all as different somewhere
else, a small town shy of pain, say, with plenty of bridges,
people hanging *Welcome Home!* banners from them

4. *Slipper or Belt*

Usual punishment was going without dinner
or Dad bending me over & tanning my cheeks red
with Mum's pink slipper. There may have been a belt
once or twice, I can't remember. Dad pushed me over
the night before my English A-level exam after I lost it,
shouting at my brothers & sister playing
as I sat the other side of the wall trying to revise.
Heard too much arrogance in my voice for his liking.

He only hit me when he thought it necessary & even then
I never felt he enjoyed it. He knew we were poor,
empathized. There was an incredible number
of people at his funeral, for a man so shy,
even when doling out punishment. They were just
trying to hold the sky together & couldn't manage the clouds

Sticks Not Twigs

It's just the drink talking,
loving the wrong person
in this pub for ten minutes

before the long walk home
& the refuse collectors
working sunrise hours.

If I could clear the banana skin
from off the pavement I would,
but you seem determined to slip

& post about these trips annually
as mini anniversaries to war endings.
My counsellor says that's your identity

as victim talking & that's comfortable
for you Mum I guess, but small Ronnie
doesn't have money for football boots

or training subs this week –
you don't mind that though, if there's
booze in the fridge, cigarettes in the house.

It's gutting, after your promising,
Ron finding water bottles filled with vodka
between cotton cumulus pillowcases.

Ronnie's taught to lose over & over
& there is nothing I can do but
smile to lighten this education.

There's something about you forever
wilting & Lord forgive me
wishing you'd just get on with it

because every night we're reduced
to cameo characters in your tragedy,
agreeing just let her have what she wants

Flights

You are only acceptable to the dysfunctional family if you follow their rules and roles. You experience rejection when you assert your needs, opinions, or desires. You lose 'love' for stepping outside your prescribed role, or telling the truth about the family's dysfunction.
— Laura K. Connell

1. Plane Window

A friend says Knock Airport
is just a shed at the end of a runway,
but leaving I spot a statue of Mary
on the tarmac for safe journeys,
blessing outgoing & incoming
travellers with her open palms:
may the flown or settling air
be made rich by your staying,
your departing. I think of Mum
who doesn't know I am flying;
it's not that she doesn't know
so much as she wouldn't think
to ask. Who am I, anyway?
How am I? Why do we sing?
The university chaplain tells me,
We're like the car & God is like the petrol,
but in His absence you have to be careful
what you fill the expanding tank with —
look, even now, this late — not listening

2. Keep It Light

Foetal alcohol spectrum disorder
is shorthand for mystery
as Mum tells me
I smoked & drank
with you, with them in
my womb. No, things
weren't good then.
I leave it there.
In exile I miss home,
the way Nanny P sweeps
through the TV guide,
licking excess ink
from her thumb.
Kebabs in her tiny
living room warm
with fairy lights & song,
my sponsored run
to the shop & back,
her leaving the lamp on.
Our own language.
In Ireland they spell
Medbh with a dee
& pretend England
isn't next door,

but wherever I am
I cannot remember
people's names,
so official policy is to
smile – it works every time

3. *Light as a Common Miracle*

You pretend your plastic bottle of spring water is not vodka.
I know.
You know I know.
I know you know I know.
You know I know you know I know.
I know you know I know you know I know.
You know I know you know I know you know I know.
I know you know I know you know I know you know I know

2

Scared animals return home, regardless of whether home is safe or frightening.

from *The Body Keeps the Score*

Working-Class Boy in a Shower Cap

Fighters are poor people. They cannot leave.
        — Bertolt Brecht

The first thing they do
when you come out
your mother's womb
is slap you pink,
welcome to the big wide
fucking world, dipstick!
Your first swim
is in the kitchen sink
with silky bubbles, fag ash
& the reams of laughter
of those you'll never forget.
Every now & then
everything aches
& a war breaks out
illustrating the truth:
might rules.
You will have to fight
one way or another,
dropped alone beside
that terrible path
of feeling your way to
God who exists
or doesn't, where
everything matters

or nothing matters.
Remember people's names,
don't be late.
Find out what keeps
you up at night
then sleep on it;
be patient;
you won't get many
chances but chances
arrive so breathe.
Do your homework;
don't be a scab.
If you're far from the sea
question the sushi;
if you're offered gum
take it because maybe
your breath stinks!
Have fun – the horizon
is always ahead of you,
even when you catch it.
Tall gardens, bulrushes,
towns with families,
new friends in green fields
wait for you as if
you are Prometheus
but with more gall;
that's if you want to leave.
It's up to you,
but boy you cannot
swim round this:

you will have to fight,
one way or another,
so tell me, what're you
gonna do about it?

The Boy Asking a Question

At first the boy
cannot ask
the question:
addressing the crowd
makes him wince,
his cheeks dimple,
his raincoat ripple,
until Pope Francis
invites him to the stage;
My son, come closer,
ask me your question,
any question,
what is on your heart?
The boy asks what a boy asks
which is never
what a man looking back
would ask but only
what a boy could ask
& that's okay.
My father was a good man,
he says, *but not baptized;*
do you think he's in heaven?
I'm reading a book
at the moment which says
adults seek mercy
while children seek justice

— wow!
When do we cross that threshold?
It was written by a friar
sitting in a library pretending
he was an oak tree, as in,
I shall not be moved
until I say This Thing;
the Pope holds the boy, says
You loved your father,
people knew him as a good man,
God would understand,
then insinuates something
off-mic about Him
not being petty
before the boy returns
to the crowd happy,
to his family,
the best people he knows

The Boy Selling Houses

Prim as a tulip
& a cousin of the wind,
moving from property
to property with few sales
but no net loss
of enthusiasm, regularly
paraphrasing joy:
here are your four walls!
here is your door,
your new neighbour,
very retired now,
so quiet you'll be able
to crack God's silence
— *at least!* —
in no time at all;
no hidden fees
or unexpected bills.
Good as my word, he says.
Gym membership.
Wax. Going to
the bar afterwards
without buying
his own cigarettes;
back to Mother's;
shagging on her
marble kitchen worktop;
same wallpaper

upstairs in his room:
dinosaurs, aggressive.
Playboy posters,
small stocks in Burberry,
severe acne at school
so feels he's owed
something,
anything really,
blueberry muffins,
loafers, nice things,
caffè macchiato,
bacon sandwiches on
Friday mornings
& when the
last block is built —
in this glass town
beside the Thames
where we were
once native —
when the last house
becomes a home
he'll get to say
I was there,
I was there

The Boy Selling Beds

Do you ever
wish you could
take a break
from being,
from existing,
pressing pause,
not dreaming,
not talking,
not looking
out of the window?
You are alive
until you are
dead, there are
no breaks.
I sell beds, say
stretch out
here, there,
this is king size,
this is queen;
the fitted
sheets for this
scoop you
together
& your body
is the cone
to a lavender

ice cream.
What happens
when there's
no more
rebellion?
Would we
recognise
goodness
if it crept
up on us
with a
hollow
bench across
its shoulders?

Bobby

It's good you're not here,
your mother says,
because there would be
too much in this world
for you to live now,
too much. How do you
mean? Bobby,
as a boy you watched
an old man running for a bus,
making it to the door
as it hauled off.
You stood & you wept
for that fella,
unaware of you,
walking stick at an obtuse
angle, panting &
wheezing in his braces

Calling Nanny P

I ring Nan
& her voice
rattles 'ello

like a half-full
box of matches,
this old Blitz girl

& I ask her
if she has been
saying her prayers?

For you I will,
she says. *I will*.
She had cursed God

after her son Bob
fell tiling a roof at
sixteen, dead.

I fuckin' hate you God
she spat in ICU,
restrained.

Bobby's blood
on the pavement,
claret, West Ham.

The smoke of London
billowing, no
progress stemmed.

Nan kept the door
handle, the last thing
he touched on

the estate before
stepping onto the bus
for work; slept with it

beneath her pillowcase,
her neck adapting to it
these thirty-odd years.

Just say hello to Him, Nan,
for me, while you can.
Will do, kid, she says,

I will, then puffs her fag

The Prince

I have a tendency to be too honourable,
but that's just me, a house like a railway station
which I'm at a loss to explain. Photograph
of a photograph of a photograph of a constant
sore for my family: Miss Roberts; Miss Roberts,
there is a thick skin that you have to have
& if I could tell anyone anything it would be that
I was shot at during the Falklands so was unable
to sweat at the time, to dance, anything profuse!
I was at Pizza Express in Woking helping myself
to Hot Honey, Pulled Lamb, Sloppy Giuseppe,
Fiorentina, Margherita, La Reine, Veneziana,
Barbacoa, Diavolo, Padana, Pollo ad Astra,
Forza, American Hot! Slice of a large Leggera.
I remember, it was as good a place as any

Dirty

Sat hanging like fresh
pasta from a coat hanger,
a young cousin
& it's my turn
to take him out for a spin,
chewing up the car park
gravel, singing his name.

His father
understands the path,
knows his son will be
in a wheelchair for life.
Mum & I buy him
a drink at the bar
where he says a true

eighteenth wouldn't
look like this, shouldn't,
that a real present
would be a visit from
a lady of the night,
the breath of a woman,
if hired, at least once
before he dies &

I'm quick to agree
as Mum leaves
with sewn-up lips
then a hiss that she
never fuckin' liked
that geezer O
Mother forgive me,
I am dirty,
I am so so dirty

Wok-A-Moley

I think I'm attracted to you
because I'm attracted to impossibility
or the possibility of failing;
& even if everything is divine,
then so is failure – the remembered
or the forgotten kind – this grease-laden
counter, these late-night noodles in a tray
committing stains over my cardigan,
this maple leaf cardigan I'll throw away

O no it was my pleasure being
so drunk with you this evening
under the orange street lamps
where cabs pull up or don't,
where the beautiful boys could
extend to hold hands but won't,
where sweet & sour dreams float
like balloons knocking heads
beneath a suspended ceiling

for Eoin K

Popular Boy

Like a year of sleep, they have
nothing to teach me, but I go,
laughing forgotten architecture.

Eleanor Roosevelt's bellboy,
dimpled as the fault lines
on a great-grandfather's atlas,

heard her song then turned
into a pillar of salt, not because
it wasn't beautiful but because

it was so tender it got translated
into great violence, cushioned
by daughters when only sons

could do, as in, take my picture
or leave. The only waitress
serving is an understudy

of how much can be wrung from
the margins of the weekend;
it is ruined, it is ruined,

we forsook the garlic so it's
ruined! Missiles of congeniality.
It's okay, if you don't love me, say

Houdini

I was the only one who knew
I was a paper draft hotel
built from nothing & how

I've moved things to suit
each guest's penchant
for the particulars.

I'll have the world
wearing a rainbow
sent up to your room?

I extinguished a candle
on a beautiful boy's shoulder blade,
haven't been the same since.

His open wound wisped,
smelled like the puddled floor
of an east Berlin flea market.

Sad guess, his brush-blond
hair swept behind his ear
as slowly as an arming

war, no, yes I was changed by it.
Girlhood is a garage band
rehearsing in the mornings

when pitter patter comes
the oncoming rain &
I'm still standing in the scene

without being there —
how may I learn this?
Let me take my turn

Toy Town

O no in big trouble again
after splintering my pool cue
over the spine of Toy Town by

telling them what I really think,
then halfway through realising
honesty is not what they asked

for or can stomach so I curtail
with long self-deprecating notes,
but already see the damage is done.

Tomorrow they'll tell shared friends
how awful I am & they'll begin with
you didn't hear this from me but how

utterly awful to say exactly what we'd both love
to say, we're fairer than he O mirror mirror . . .
The seagulls here are bigger than toddlers!

The stream drawbridge is baked-oak brown &
its string tangs like the stick-end of sellotape.
The Poet Laureate of Toy Town reluctantly

gives a reading & we all reluctantly attend,
but the Laureate seems particularly sad
today so I say this poet is depressed;

O no in big trouble again . . .

Juliet Says to Her Nurse, the City is a Bruise

after Walter Sickert

I fall in love with those in love with love
every relationship is a history of the Uzi
as in bang bang bang nothing left moving
here are my demons here are my demands

I want to make it wiping tables in a fast-food restaurant
I want to comb my hair waiting on the inevitable to happen
I want to find the paintings from the hallways of my youth
I want my Romeo who wants to set fire to everything

then I threw my grief like a knife into the ocean
no waves were harmed so I bought a new knife
I know the root of my fear is in surrendering
without regard for any of the consequences

O Girl

I was only
trying to tell you
something to make
you feel good
when you finished
reading your poem
— I said *that was
read confidently*
O girl you said
*confidently as in
not very good?*
The truth is
I did not like
your poem no
you were
disparaging
about a Wilko
or the people
shopping in Wilko
& if not
disparaging
at least too ironic
so I did not like
your poem
but I was trying
to be nice
because I want

people to leave
me feeling better
than when they
met me that's
how we unfuck
the world
by healing
one person
at a time
O girl you
just thought I
was condescending

Brahms & Liszt

Her football team wore all black, kicked & spat like mourners, & had sleepovers where they spooned across mattresses, replaying Saddam Hussein hanged online with the hosting girl returning with square pizza boxes & two-litre bottles of coke. They ate marshmallows scorched by the lighter of their rotund goalkeeper who smoked, who had her belly button pierced & played with one hand covering her abdomen at all times. She enjoyed hitting the grass a little more than saving the ball, but not by much. Most of the girls in the team were gay. Mostly they loved each other as sisters, each now having more than one set of parents.

One evening my sister came home completely gazeboed from the clubhouse so I sat up most of the night outside her door or by her bed because Mum was trying to come in & tear off her head. This was the punch-drunk double-header of her daughter being newly unlikely to deliver them heirs & J being as sloshed as Mum was then. After untangling nicotined fingers from out my sister's hair, I cleared a chair & sat until she fell asleep. *Just don't become like me*, I heard Mum blub upstairs, *don't become whatever you do like me;*

the young Brahms looked back to what was before & trailing him, but the elder Liszt watched for the future coming down the road, a novella on the economics of conflict in his fawn trench coat. O the bus windows steamed up by the breath of angels! Wagner was their mutual love, a bridge on which the two musicians met: one artist recognizing another as sister.

I hadn't remembered acting the knight that night until J mentioned it after it surfacing with her counsellor — that's how normal it all was: you forget the individual bombs, bullets or duds during the war stuck on loop, where truth is not the first casualty, it's one's reverence for the truth. But when I did make it out to university, the women there greeted me with *you just don't understand* & *how could you*

The Girl Who Grew up to Drive Ambulances

These are your lights now
flashing blue over streets
where you kicked footballs
where your mother
drove you to school
past the shopping trolleys

languishing in the pond
having made sure
you had brushed your teeth
brushed your hair now dyed
candy-floss pink
softer with every rinse

your ambulance partner
is unbearably into Shania Twain
in a very unrealistic way
has a cardboard cutout
on the first-floor balcony of her flat
she survives exclusively on pizza

margherita topped with cold coleslaw
a hill you know she will die on
fighting your brothers for the last slice
one night shift she beautifully explained
the evolution of the word silly
formerly signifying holiness

because silly once meant holy
it came to mean righteous
because silly meant righteous
it came to mean noble
because silly meant noble
it came to mean innocent

innocent came to mean harmless
harmless to mean helpless
helpless to mean ignorant
ignorant to mean childish
childish came to mean goofy
absolute goofball like you! she says

for my sister, J

Sweeper

Don't flinch, the ring on my necklace was relegated
after my smallest sister bought me another sweeper
from the Argos catalogue with the money she earned
working in a butcher's over Christmas — just imagine! —
all those meaty men who happily proclaimed themselves
swingers & ate cheese rolls at break times but there were
no break times; she says her hands smelled of Fairy Liquid
for weeks & now she can't go near the stuff or even wash up.
This is all to say if you buy me a necklace without a crucifix
I am unlikely to wear it; it's not that I will sell it or anything,
but once you've found your cross you bear it & sometimes
that means staying, growing old within your home town,
where lungs understand the tick of air in the summer,
where *Be My Regret?* is tattooed onto loins

But & Though

Archangel Gabriel invented butterflies,
but tragedy continues as if the skies

were empty, though our sisters are besties,
always round each other's houses

& being unwilling to step on the gaps
between pavement slabs, walk to school

supporting each other's arms. The sun across
their burgundy jumpers is a moving painting,

the almond branches above them welcome the wind.
I can no longer pirouette around our fractured values

said my sister to yours, who laughed in response,
said shut up & let's go to the new donuts place.

They'll walk home fast to speak over the phone.
There's never any news so they make their own

3

*You have made us for yourself,
and our heart is restless until it rests in you.*

– Saint Augustine

Happy Hour

Time slips away, but does it all get easier or do we just lower our expectations? Is growing up a series of compromises; is resistance brave or stupid? The doctor says, between a baguette & her next patient, the symptoms of alcohol delirium exhibit themselves similarly to the symptoms of an infection, but we can't locate an infection so we can't say for sure. Take a seat in the family room, there's a vending machine outside the door.

Mum's hair is conker brown, clumpy & matted where she's been busy with the French Resistance fighting Nazi occupation — *Them bloody bastards are bombing our chip shops!* — so the nurses have stopped touching her & started calling these delusions her baseline. Nanny P says Mum's been having fisticuffs with the orderlies & nurses. In the video my brother messages me, Mum's head bops to unheard music as she tends a bar, puffs a gap in the pair of fingers rising to her lips & asks if he fancies some lemonade or peanuts. We're at the clubhouse; we're back to where I emptied ashtrays for a pound a pop & Tom took a record-breaking shit in the camp we made outside from three tarped-together trees. Onomatopoeia is the full Shakespearean play for the single word plop. I see the green of the football being played on the screen inside, its reflection in the bronze bar. I can smell pork scratchings, their sting & cut of gums. The video records Mum's last moments, a scene I have lived to expect though could never prepare for. We spend the days believing she is about to die.

It's a Herculean effort to let go of someone you love & for a long time that's all I learned, how great that effort is. Once I envied a girl whose mother is dead for the neatness of such a rupture. Mum's a ghost who needs driving to the hospital & feeling sorry for. She believes witnessing many people gathered round her bed will be the cure, but if we could love her back to full strength she would already be having breakfast with Lazarus at a table with gulls overhead & the hush of waves breaking at the end of the lane. Nothing will change until she loves herself again. Who can rob you of this talent? Nan says the nurses have been throwing Mum in & out of her bed like a bundle of clothes.

After a week, Mum's washed & nurses call her a completely different person. The timeline matches alcohol delirium, we are told, but we can't say for sure. Her confusion may have been the expression of a malign, undetected infection; furthermore, though damage to the brain's memory – as scans show – is currently reversible, this will progress if drinking continues. If your mother does not stop consuming alcohol, this state of delirium may even become permanent, like dementia, like misremembering who she is. Mum stays optimistic, humbly accepts, then returns to where her very existence creates smiles for miles & miles & light years

The Present

I smashed a plate because my hand was slippy & two days later I still haven't hoovered the shards. If I label this celebration, is that what it is? Why do I write better in my boxers? I dress better when I have ten minutes to get ready; I enjoy myself more when the cab's outside & I'm still not packed.

This Christmas is the first we'll spend together without a single person drinking under your roof – for the best, I think, everything is so fragile. You ask me to pick up instant coffee on my way to yours – 'all-in-one cappuccinos', whatever that means – & this is your new thing, six or seven cups a day; you can't sleep but that's tomorrow's problem, for a future you. The Big Book says, one day at a time. In modern parlance, keep it simple, stupid!

This will be our first Jesus's birthday without you slurring after 3 p.m. I've marked this by writing you a poem & titling it with a name my fiancée will not allow me to save for our children. I buy a pink frame just the right side of deranged. In our poetry workshops, I draw different faces in pencil over friends' drafts by way of cheerleading. On crisp archival paper, my face for you is in permanent blue ink with spit marks coming from its mouth towards the body of words. You unwrap & read from the neon frame in your wheelchair.

Before Gazza scored in Euro 96, he placed a bottle of water beside Scotland's goal in his uncut certainty of scoring, of peeling Wembley's roof off. If you rotate the still of Gazza's celebration ninety degrees it becomes a Crucifixion scene with water flowing in the opposite direction. I study a poet at university – the body of her poem is altered by the action of its images like a moving staircase or a briefcase left on a tube finding a new life within the lost & found department. Why wouldn't my stanzas bleed into one another? People leave things behind when they're drunk, but life is movement & maybe one day I'll sleep again at your house, Mum. Still under construction, how do we toast to your achievement? With instant coffee from Poundland

Booby Trap

I tripped on the wire of the city
& all of the lights cut out;

restored, they held an action replay
& said it was entirely my fault.

Mercy to whom I have undone,
all they may undo. Please know

my sadness is fraught with hindsight;
I was once a great mirror boy! Now

I am just a yo-yo that's given up,
a heart bled into a white tablecloth.

Drive-by laughter at the bus stop:
you're the schmuck who tripped

the power, you think you're better
than us. No, please, it was an accident.

Best of luck fighting on every
front says history always

Spaghetti Western, Alphabetti Spaghetti, Spaghetti to Forgetti Your Regretti, Spaghetti & a Whole Fist

This time last year you were in hospital due to an unfathomable infection. Turns out, you were admitted after being scooped up from the living room floor by a neighbour with a life-threatening percentage of alcohol in your system. It was the night of Lenny's wedding anniversary party – something not about you. You must have fallen. Mum as verb. Mum as one steaming hot bowl of excuses with cracked pepper & Parmesan. Say when. When when when. You must have asked the doctors & nurses to keep information from us so when we questioned, the empty two-litre bottle of vodka rolled away from your wheelchair was not part of the scene or story. You could not be in the throes of withdrawal if you hadn't even been drinking. Denial makes you hostile when we press; bad sons, disloyal sons & daughters. As soon as the war is over & relative peace returns, the last thing anyone wants to do is talk about the still-recent war because that would be risking everything. You really would be a turncoat then. Even your own brothers can turn on you. So when I suggest rehab or committed, long-term counselling & none of this a-few-NHS-sessions-here-&-there nonsense, half a year on a waiting list, my words are met as if I'm a bully. She's doing okay, let her be; stop being hard on her. But & though & maybe tomorrow

*

Ostracism is the subtlest form of bullying, where action can be camouflaged as inaction. Not one person in the history of humanity has ever bullied their way to a better world. Evangeline Booth, born on Christmas Day in South Hackney, rode a hay wagon through the morning streets of New York City collecting the confused, the dry wisps & heavy-set regrets back onto the wagon bound for the Salvation Army mission

*

The hospital isn't getting back to you about your hip operation so you drink & gulp in bed & there is no healing. I only notice you're back on it when your voice sounds different yet familiar over the phone. Aunties say *Well it's her life* & I will wonder where Ophelia's friends were when she headed for the stream, if Ophelia's only ever noticed by her absence, like missing a hair appointment. Drowning in lily water seems awfully posh compared with walking to the corner shop & buying the cheapest bottle of vodka or sending your sons up the high road for mixer. I never came back with orange juice, always spent the money on something else & never did myself any favours by refusing. After all these years, whatever I do or don't do you just want to be left alone to do this in peace, to blow in the breeze of whatever is coming. Maybe only in heaven will you remember that I remembered you

*

My counsellor says, acceptance is forgiveness without hierarchy, whereas the word forgive implies a debt overlooked. None of us are good enough for each other & that's exactly why we're all good enough for each other. Martin Luther King Jr. says forgiveness is an attitude. It will, it will all be different this time. Okay, how? It will, it will. But how will it be different though? I just needed it, I just needed it. What exactly will be different? You don't believe I like you. I love you. But do you mean it though? You don't know how much I want to trust you, to just hold your hand while walking round Tesco. I don't need your recovery, for you to get it right, just for you to try

*

It's not what has happened to you, it's not how it has happened to you, it's how you feel about what has happened to you. Twin brothers can experience the same thing & one finish with a smile on their face & the other with a knife in their hand. Acceptance is largely a silent practice, something maybe only God can hear

*

Jesus was asked how many times one should forgive a brother & he replied, somewhat cheekily, seventy times seven. Seventy times seven is 490, but I'm lowering my head bracing for the 491st with you, mother; that's God's completely sensible irrational forgiveness at work where even crashing together can be communion. How generous is . . . are you still there?

The Passover

I still imagine you jumping Double Dutch
over gruff Brummy pavement atop bubble-gum
knees before being sent round the roundabout
to fetch the priest: Spaghetti Junction's complete
& the Irish labourers wish for its blessing.
Prayer is floating, looping between concrete.
God bless all who may pass over this structure.
Let this new feat of man be for the benefit of all.
There is dancing, there is singing in the street,
there is toothpaste on your chin no one sees
as you stand watching the parades go by.
A cinema of myrtles on the roundabout across
is itself a church without flags or broken promises,
sacred to you but you can't find the words
in an England where a girl was meant to be seen
not believed. All these keepers of the faith,
& not one of them asked who hurt you

Silent Prayer in Eau Claire

People shovel snow together during the winter,
giving them an excuse to talk more,
to keep away from the big cities,
to be each other's keeper

even from the back seat of a car
you can see their breath spelling
all luxuries are in the end only
democratic paper plates – humble,
paling, caring histories undeclared

that sacrifice is the opposite of comfort
or comfort is the opposite of sacrifice,
the sound rain might make in reverse
if you'd never cried a single day

there is a bus stop beside the depot
where Christ was glimpsed a starving bride
wearing something new & something old
in sandy pink plimsolls – no longer
a delicate boy but still the poem of God

where every few days a new bouquet is taped
to the side of the road & when a fresh
arrangement is made, fading daffodils,
carnations, roses, tulips are slung backwards

to folk who have borrowed their love,
who pray for those who wish them harm,
they make the catch or they don't,
someone does, someone doesn't,
the bus to work then the bus home

Potluck

I flipped burgers with a firework
from the soul of the doorway

    unfortunately,
like running out into a motorway
to lay cones for ensuing roadworks.

Swerving varicose veins. Pizza nipples.

Courageous is such a courageous word,
don't you find? Sculptural in its qualities.
My tongue wants a reason to say it,
but the heart needs a reason.

Freud says it's not the pain of falling
that stings so much as the confusion
of having fallen. Hercules knows the pain
of being away from home for too long.

Took me thirty years to know preventing
your death is not a power in my hands;
drunk is the only way that you can live.

Severe is persevere's majority shareholder

The Understudies

Love gives up moonlighting as noun to be the verb,
so much for everyone else & never enough for itself
as carpenters, secretaries, dinner ladies, key cutters,
the woman at the mortgage shop taking a cigarette
every morning behind the maroon square building
to turn silver ringlets into the sky – each may declare
they believe in nothing, zilch, nada, naked nihilism,
but if each rose today how can that be completely
true? I'm not arguing they believe in a fluffy God
or his son who lost it only once, riding on lambs'
backs between the legs of fountain coin-tossers,
but I feel it – can't you? These glorious people
really aren't convinced by the opposite either.
Keep your heart the understudy of another

Glint of Promise

I threw 10p into a well,
making a wish that my life
would always be difficult,
knowing the diamond of me
could not be fully formed
if everything was easy-peasy-
lemon-squeezy all the time

I still believe this is the only wish
God ever intervened to grant me,
seeing a boyish reflection
as I did from the top lip
of the well, promise

later I developed a terrible habit,
a terrible habit I won't go into here –
despite miles & miles of contrary efforts,
why is it we change right at the precipice,
when the enemy is at our black gate,
when it feels like there's nothing
left to defend but a tatty bridge
to a self we can no longer love
or care to maintain?

if the light of God
does not let darkness remain,
how does transformation arrive
so late in the day, so improbably,
like sunlight hitting a wristwatch
on the other side of a lake,
changing everything

The Professional Peanut Butter Taster

The sun has marked the lines of her tee
onto her neck & arms, uncertain
as a baby rhyme mistakenly
swapped in a neonatal ward
& taken home to only chances.

Her father saved a pension with
the Royal Canadian Mounted,
but was built for professional ice
hockey like an unpainted wooden
staircase up to unemployment offices.

This peanut butter, she says finally,
is the time between lightning &
thunder. & that peanut butter,
said firmly, is a river of retirement

speeches, as in, please, just get on with it
& go home & paint like you promised.
The wind has set up school here
without a curriculum, but I will name
my first daughter Harper. I will tell her,

my love, somewhere in the world
a poet is sitting down to write;
a pastry sous chef is rubbing
sleep from an eye; one lover
is inking a hymn to another
just because it's a Tuesday. Listen,

the taste of hope is a new friend
laughing on the street below
with its echo reaching up
to your open window. Harper!
Hold it open as long as you can.
Outwards from joy, my love,
never backwards from fear

We Disagree on Sabrina for a Girl

We have these great big bay windows
looking out over the sea, & the ferry exchange
for Cairnryan can be seen floating every morning.

All the people about to board, fishing out tickets
from pockets with cold, reluctant fingers.
I sit & watch your slow movement with coffee.

These windows mist over every evening
when we're frying something or draining pasta.
It's a peace I've never known before,

a peace that's never met me before,
but I can feel it learning my name, my lean.
On Friday I wait home for an engagement ring

to be delivered to our door, hide it in the attic.
Lilies have such longevity as dying flowers:
I bought them when we moved here

& their heads have grown proud & stately.
I make dinner & these dark windows fog again.
Sometimes the blue lapping against them

is urgent like puffs of neon octopuses
floating up to say hi,
squishing their noses up to the panes.

Turns out, there's a nursing home next door —
ambulance blue means half of something like us
is dying tonight. They'd tell us to enjoy the view

Friday Night Drift

You get home & my heart
leaps then rolls like a vast
brass band marching through town

*

The working week has worn you through,
so you sleep lightly in the nook
between my collarbone
& the crest of my chest,
raising your head
every now & then to ask,
I can't hear your heartbeat?
Can you help me take my earrings off?

Pinocchio is a real boy thus a liar,
but my love, would I do anything to prevent
damaging your innocent outlook,
even if it meant keeping a secret or two
from you? My love, of course.
Every old ship is surely allowed its secrets.

Would I read poems to our child
while you carried them to term?
My love, of course. Would I fight for you
until a bloody death? Yes, & I would walk the plank . . .

but I'm not explaining the bloody plot again
if you can't keep your droopy eyes open!
O my darling, we've half-watched so many
dramas by now, imagining our own conclusions.

I google the synonyms for acceptance:
receipt, receiving, taking, obtaining, undertaking,
welcoming, embracing, approval, adoption;
I'm surprised by the number of doing words,
I'm surprised acceptance doesn't have any real family.

What was the name of the film we watched
about the landlady who gets married
to the sailor who spoke a great metaphor for love?
I must have been sleeping, you say.
Yes I remember – his sailor friend asks him why he stays
& he surveys the sea before declaring something like,
because I'm just a small, flawed boat in the terrific blue
& when we docked at this port, I liked it here,
they'll say there are better ports but I really like it here

Saturday

In a sweater your grandmother knitted aboard
HMS Something-or-other, you don't believe
in giving custom to shops out of yellow HB pencils;
you believe Satan is a freedom fighter seeing as angels
are obliged to walk the line, to sit in their hot seats
answering questions & praying for the worrisome,
which is to say you find the whole idea of praying beside
thrones all day long a little boring & I understand that.
Well I understand but I fear a failure of the imagination
& I'm not above the millions who have died with such hope.
Three women by Botticelli in a circle joining fingers,
auburn hair & pale muslin dress – a way of seeing
the world & interviewing it. Your lisp is the splash
of raindrops over every fence & parliament building
as we hold hands between market stalls. You say I dress
like Johnny Knoxville's little brother, protracted firework.
Saturdays smelling the flowers, learning their names,
buttering the bread & making it up as we go along.
We are all we will have to show for it. I love you

For My Daughter to Come

The song you sing beside the river
        is breakfast for the grass but homework

for the policeman, the palace & the prince
        as a continent of vending machines

dispenses peaches into milksop throats;
        the song is always about being alone

because that is what is known instinctively &
        singing together makes one less lonely.

There is always a layer of atoms between
        the piano stool & the pockmarked carpet,

the can of spinach & the muscles of Popeye,
        the hazel hair of Christ as He sweeps

a waterfall of locks behind His ear:
        one object never actually touches another,

but there are no atoms between the Father &
        the Son, between the Holy Spirit & you –

your song is God's sweet experience of this world:
        unique, irreplaceably part of the whole

Birthday Suicide Letter

I have been so used to you being dead
that when I got the text saying you had
swallowed fifty paracetamol with a bottle,
I went about things as normal: I thanked
the driver with a wave as I stepped off the bus;
smiled at the ticket inspector singing Whitney's
I wanna feel the heat with somebody!
while baking & breathing in the air of the city,
before remembering Lewisham's young Ella.
I said a little prayer as I sat in the cemetery
across from the hospital, its tiny chapel still
under tarp & scaffolding. Mum's in the loneliest
place in the world but surrounded by people
anxious at her bed, the people she would have
anticipated turning up for this call this time.
If heaven can be right now then so can
its opposite also – every wave of the sea,
every crest, trough & distance between.
Halfway through she phoned her friend
who phoned the paramedics who pumped
her stomach, all within her birthday hours.
The ambulance crew took her letter
& never explained its contents to us;
I imagine it's a ta-la to this cruel world
as all her birthday cards sat unopened.
We aren't designed to live detached,

but I accept I cannot take any more.
That's okay, this is an act of love too;
so when the doctor asks us who is the
next of kin, I let someone else speak

NOTES & ACKNOWLEDGEMENTS

The epigraph is from Roy M. Liuzza's translation of 'Dream of the Rood' (Anon), poetryfoundation.org.

Section 2 epigraph is from *The Body Keeps the Score* by Bessel van der Kolk (Viking, 2014).

Section 3 epigraph is from Saint Augustine's *Confessions*, translated by Henry Chadwick (OUP, 1991).

'Fathers & Sons' is after Tom Leonard's poem of the same title.

'Dad's still in a coma so I'm sent' references Seamus Heaney's 'Clearances'.

'Off the Back of a Lorry' references Isaiah 32:2 and the eleven rock-hewn churches close to the town of Lalibela, Ethiopia.

'Sticks Not Twigs' shares its title with a song by The Cribs.

The first section of 'Flights' references Ecclesiastes 3:11. The quotation by Laura K. Connell is from www.laurakconnell.com.

'Working-Class Boy in a Shower Cap' alludes to Charles Bukowski's 'The Laughing Heart'. The epigraph is taken from Bertolt Brecht's poem 'There is no greater crime than leaving', translated by Frank Jones.

'The Boy Asking a Question' references the book *Alive in God: A Christian Imagination* by Timothy Radcliffe (Bloomsbury, 2019) and is a play on a conversation held between Pope Francis and a member of his audience.

'Bobby' and 'Calling Nanny P' are in memory of Robert Terence Hawkey, 1966–1982.

'The Prince' is a collage and bricolage of Prince Andrew's words in a 2019 BBC interview with Emily Maitlis.

'Juliet Says to her Nurse, the City Is a Bruise' is after Walter Sickert's painting 'Juliet and her Nurse', 1935–6.

'The Girl Who Grew Up to Drive Ambulances' references the article 'The Fascinating Evolution of the Word Silly' by Spencer McDaniel.

'But & Though' references Conservative MP Victoria Atkins's words upon her resignation as a minister from Boris Johnson's government in 2022.

'Spaghetti Western . . .' references Matthew 18:21–2 in its final section.

'Friday Night Drift' references a film – involving a conversation between sailors – the title of which I genuinely cannot remember.

'For My Daughter to Come' is after 'To an Unborn Daughter' by Jen Herron.

'Birthday Suicide Letter' refers to Ella Adoo-Kissi-Debrah (2004–2013), a young girl from south London who became the first person in the world to have air pollution listed as cause of death on her death certificate. The line 'I wanna feel the heat with somebody!' is from the song 'I Wanna Dance With Somebody', lyrics © Boy Meets Girl Music, Irving Music Inc.

An earlier version of 'Dad's still in a coma so I'm sent' is published in *Hold Open the Door: Commemorative Anthology from the Ireland Chair of Poetry* (UCD, 2020). My thanks to *Agape Review* for publishing 'Glint of Promise'. Cheers to the editors of *The Blue Nib* and *The Honest Ulsterman* for publishing earlier versions of 'Lenny' and 'We Disagree on Sabrina for a Girl'. I am grateful to

Lumpen for publishing my chapbook *Breeze Block* (2020), which features some of the poems in this book, often in earlier forms.

I am very grateful for the love, work, support and encouragement of my family, Emma, and Emma's family, especially John and Liz. My love always to my friends William Lailey, Joshua F. Dias, John Hoggett, and Christopher Hubble. I am extremely grateful for the work and diligence of my editor, Colette Bryce, who, in the bringing of this book together, no doubt saved me many times from myself. My mighty thanks to Nick Laird for guiding me in the earliest versions of these poems. I am grateful to Eoin Kelly, who read countless drafts of many of these poems and made them better. I am grateful to Berhane and Alem for their spiritual stewardship. Many thanks to Brian, who I credit for 'the horizon is always ahead of you, even when you catch it.'

Thanks to my fellow artists, writers, teachers, and co-ordinators, those who have helped and inspired me during the writing of this book, particularly Stuart Cumberland, Roy McFarlane, John F. Deane, Matthew Rice, Adrian Rice, Sally Read, Matthew McGlinchey, Pete Owen, Bebe Ashley, Philip Lee, Rachel Brown, Charles Lang, Scott McKendry, Charlie McIlwain, Alanna Offield, Johnny Keating, Stuart Horner, Zara Meadows, Mícheál McCann, Supriya Kaur Dhaliwal, Marcella L.A. Prince, J. Taylor Bell, Paul Maddern, Medbh McGuckian, Ian Sansom, Stephen Sexton, Leontia Flynn, Dorothy Spencer, Fran Lock, Milena Williamson, and Padraig Regan. Cheers to all current and former Queen's University, Belfast and SHC staff for sharing their encouraging zeal and wisdom.

A special thanks to the Irish Department for the Economy (DfE) for their financial support of these poems which began as the creative component of a PhD project. This book wasn't inevitable and this collection was made possible through the awarding of this funding, allowing me the time and space to write.

The cover of this book features a painting by Marilyn Swann (1932–2018), a talented artist from Bexleyheath whose work I stumbled across under strange circumstances – but that's a story for another time.

Godspeed to all who believed in this project from the beginning and went above and beyond in helping me put it together during its different phases. If I've missed some names, here's to the unacknowledged legislators of the world – salut!